Escape to Freedom: The Underground Railroad

by Barbara Brooks Simons

Table of Contents

Pictures To Think About	i
Words To Think About	iii
Introduction	2
Chapter 1 The Underground Railroad	6
Chapter 2 Resisting Slavery	12
Chapter 3 All Aboard!	18
Chapter 4 Heroes of the Underground Railroad	24
Conclusion	30
Glossary	31
Index	32

Pictures To Think About

Escape to Freedom: The Underground Railroad

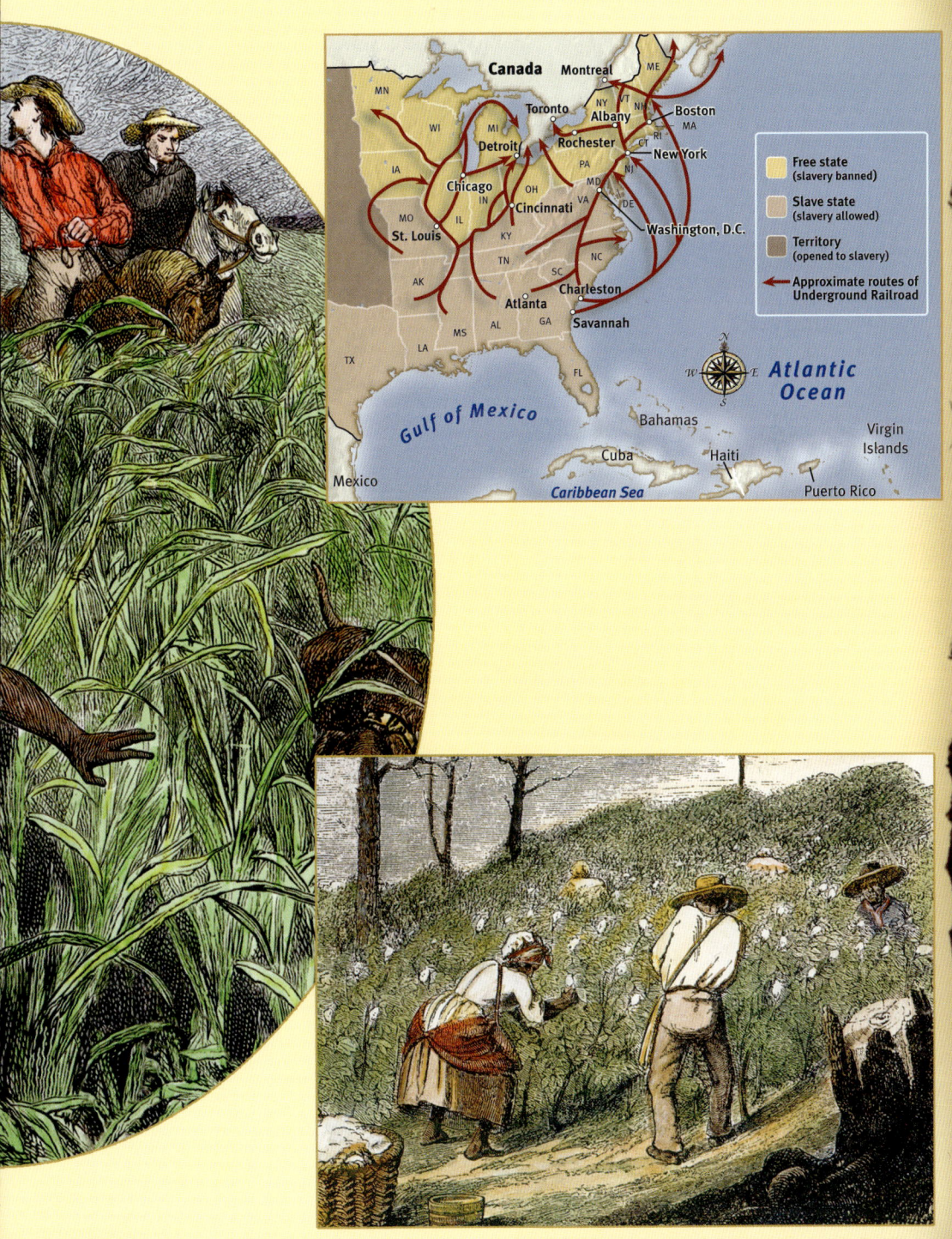

Words To Think About

Characteristics

- type of song
- sung by slaves
- ?

Examples

- "Swing Low, Sweet Chariot"
- "Go Down, Moses"
- ?

spiritual

What do you think the word **spiritual** means?

abolitionist

What do you think the word **abolitionist** means?

Who was an abolitionist?
- free black people
- ?
- former slaves

What did an abolitionist do?
- helped slaves escape
- ?
- worked to end slavery

iii

Read for More Clues
abolitionist, page 6
conductor, page 8
spiritual, page 22

conductor

What do you think the word **conductor** means in this book?

Meaning 1
leader of an orchestra or band
(noun)

Meaning 2
person who works for a railroad
(noun)

Meaning 3
substance that can transmit heat and electricity
(noun)

iv

Introduction

▲ Men, women, and children were bought and sold at auction.

In 1619, a Dutch ship sailed to Jamestown, Virginia. A group of Africans went ashore. They were the first Africans to arrive in the colonies. The first Africans in the colonies were **indentured servants** (ihn-DEHN-chuhrd SUHR-vuhnts). This type of servant worked for a number of years. Then the servant was set free.

But in time, life changed for black servants. In 1705, the Virginia colony passed a new law. The law said that blacks were slaves for life. Slaves were property. A slave could be bought and sold like land. Other colonies also had laws like this.

People began to capture African men, women, and children. They brought Africans to the colonies on slave ships. Then they sold the Africans as slaves. Slavery became a business.

▲ An indentured servant usually worked for seven years and then was freed.

INTRODUCTION

Most slaves were sold in the South. Southern planters grew crops on huge farms called **plantations** (plan-TAY-shuhnz). Plantations needed many slaves to work in the fields. Some slaves were carpenters or blacksmiths. Others cooked and cleaned.

Slavery was awful. The work was hard. Children were taken from parents and sold. Owners could be cruel. Most slaves dreamed of being free.

In 1776, the United States became a country. By 1800, some states had outlawed slavery. These "free states" were in the North.

▲ Cotton plantations used many enslaved workers.

▲ The United States grew as new states entered the Union. The big question was, would the new states be slave states or free states? The debate over slavery split the country.

Many slaves wanted to escape. Some brave people in free states wanted to help. They started the Underground Railroad, or UGRR.

In this book, you will read about the UGRR. You will see how the UGRR helped thousands escape slavery.

CHAPTER 1

The Underground Railroad

The Underground Railroad was not a real railroad. It was a secret group of people. These people wanted to abolish, or end, slavery. They were called **abolitionists** (a-buh-LIH-shuhn-ihsts). Some members were free black people. Some members were former slaves. Other members were white people. They all risked their lives to help slaves escape. They hid slaves in their homes and barns. They helped **fugitives** (FYOO-jih-tihvz), or runaway slaves, travel many miles.

The Underground Railroad began in the 1830s. It had hundreds, maybe thousands, of safe houses. The railroad had many escape routes. All routes led to the free states in the North. Many people living in Northern states protected runaway slaves.

Primary Source

Abolitionists felt very strongly about the issue of slavery. Here is a quote from Mr. Lyman Goodnow, an abolitionist:
"We were very radical, however, in our views of right and wrong.... We opposed bad men everywhere, supported all fugitive slaves who came to us, and worked like beavers for the right."

◀ Most slaves were not allowed to learn to read. Runaways had no maps or directions. They traveled at night with only the North Star as their guide.

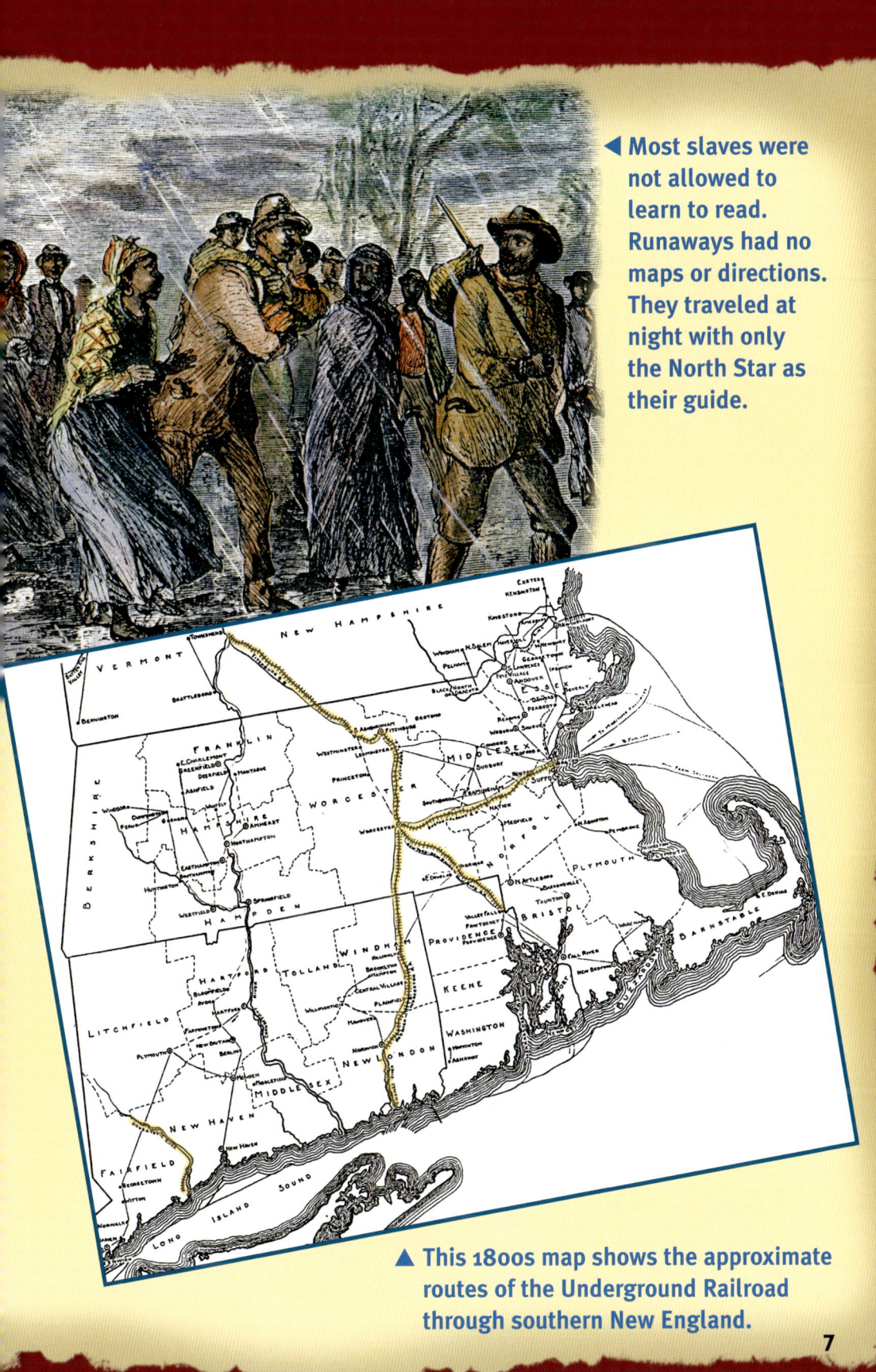

▲ This 1800s map shows the approximate routes of the Underground Railroad through southern New England.

7

CHAPTER 1

How the UGRR Worked

People who worked for the Underground Railroad were called "agents." Agents sent messages in code. They used real railroad terms. Runaway slaves were "parcels," or packages. A **conductor** (kuhn-DUHK-tuhr) took "parcels" to **stations**, or safe houses. Slaves hid in attics and cellars. Then they moved on. Some stations had rooms behind fake walls. Other homes had secret passages. Fugitives could escape quickly.

A safe house owner was a **stationmaster**. He and his family hid runaways. They also gave the runaways food and comfort.

▲ The best time for slaves to escape was at night under the cover of darkness.

THE UNDERGROUND RAILROAD

Runaways were scared, cold, and tired. Often, runaways walked barefoot for weeks or months. At the station, they found hot meals and warm blankets.

The stationmaster passed messages between conductors. He also sent information to other stations. Friends might help by lending wagons to carry slaves to the next station. Local men donated shoes and suits. Women sewed shirts and dresses. With new clothes, runaway slaves looked like free people. That made escape easier.

Eyewitness Account

William Still was a free black man. Still was an active abolitionist. He lived in Philadelphia. In 1850, he became head of a group there. The group gave fugitives food, shelter, money, and legal help. Still kept careful records and made notes about his "passengers." In his book about the Underground Railroad, he told some of their stories:

"Sam said he left because his master threatened to sell him . . . But this was not all. Sam declared his master had threatened to shoot him a short while before he left . . . . Charles offered the same excuse as did Sam. He had been threatened with the auction-block. He left his mother free, but four sisters he left in chains . . . . They were all young men, hale and stout, with strong resolutions to make Canada their future home."

CHAPTER 1

At least 3,000 people were Underground Railroad "agents." Most worked in secret. Very few kept records. They did not want records to fall into the hands of slave catchers.

It was dangerous to be an agent. Angry slave owners attacked some agents. Others had agents arrested.

Talk About It

Tell a partner about some of the responsibilities of UGRR agents. Then talk about the personal traits or qualities the agents demonstrated by doing this dangerous work.

▲ Agents and slave catchers battled each other. If caught, agents could lose their lives.

THE UNDERGROUND RAILROAD

Underground Railroad Routes

Most UGRR agents worked in the free states. Some brave agents worked in the "borderland." This was the land along the Ohio River. The river formed the northern border of Kentucky. Kentucky was a slave state. Conductors met slaves at night. Then they took the slaves across the river to the free state of Ohio.

Many routes led to port cities on the Great Lakes. From there, fugitives could take "abolition boats" to Canada. Slavery was illegal in Canada.

In 1850, the Fugitive Slave Law was passed. The law let slave catchers bring fugitives in free states back to slave states. As a result, thousands of fugitives went to Canada.

11

CHAPTER 2

Resisting Slavery

Slaves had very hard lives. They wanted freedom. Some slaves rebelled. They fought slave owners. In states with many slaves, white people feared slave **uprisings** (UHP-ry-zihngz).

Before the UGRR, thousands of slaves ran away on their own. Most were young, strong men. Running away was dangerous and sometimes deadly. Many tried and failed.

▲ Angry owners sent out slave catchers with guns and fierce dogs to find runaways.

Math Matters

Slaveholders hated the UGRR. They thought it robbed them of valuable property. In Washington, D.C. and northern Virginia, for example, a strong young field worker was priced at about $350 in 1800. By 1853, the average price had risen to $1,250—an increase of almost four times.

Owners punished runaway slaves harshly. Still, some slaves ran away again and again. Freedom was worth the risk.

Views of Slavery

Many people were against slavery. But slavery had supporters as well. Some slave owners thought that African Americans could not look after themselves. The owners believed that slaves needed them for food and shelter. Many songs told of happy slaves singing and dancing. The truth was that most slaves were not happy at all.

In My Opinion

George Fitzhugh was a Virginia lawyer. His view of slavery was shared by many in the South. Slaves would have strongly disagreed with Fitzhugh's ideas:
"The Negro slaves of the South are the happiest, and in some sense, the freest people in the world. The children and the aged and the infirm work not at all, and yet have all the comforts and necessities of life provided to them. . . . The women do little hard work . . . The Negro men and stout boys work, on the average and in good weather, not more than nine hours a day."

William Wells Brown was a fugitive slave. After his escape, he wrote a book about his life as a slave. His autobiography was an instant best seller. It sold more than ten thousand copies in two years. This is an excerpt:
"We have here before us a cotton plantation with slaves picking cotton. The usual task for a man is eighty pounds per day; for a woman, seventy pounds; but they often work them far above this task. During the task time, if a slave fails to accomplish this task, he receives five cuts with the cat-o-nine tails, or the negro whip, for every pound of cotton that is wanting to make up the requisite number."

CHAPTER 2

▼ The book *Uncle Tom's Cabin* changed the way many people viewed slavery.

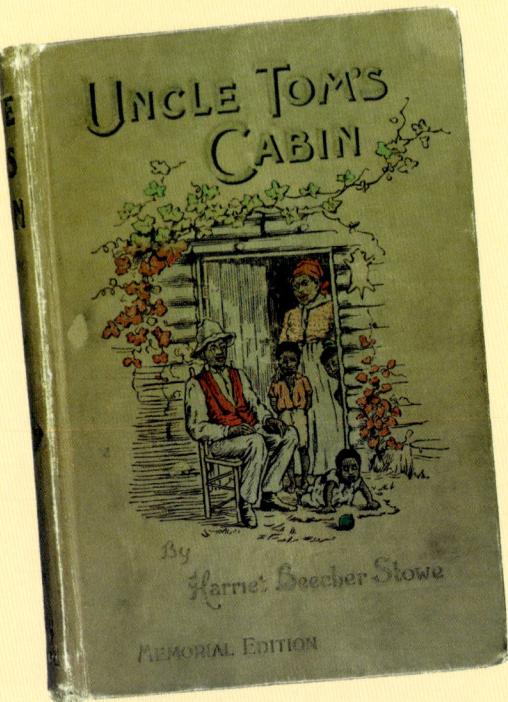

THEY MADE A DIFFERENCE

Harriet Beecher Stowe

Harriet Beecher Stowe was born in New England. She came from a family of abolitionists. While living in Ohio, she saw fleeing slaves pass through her home. UGRR conductors and stationmasters told her stories. She also visited friends on a plantation across the river in Kentucky. In 1863, during the Civil War, Stowe met President Abraham Lincoln. Legend says that he greeted her by saying, "So you're the little woman who wrote the book that made this great war?"

In the North, most people did not think about slavery. Then, in 1852, a novel shook people up. The book was called *Uncle Tom's Cabin*. It was written by Harriet Beecher Stowe. The book was a best seller. It was translated into more than thirty languages. It was read all over the world.

RESISTING SLAVERY

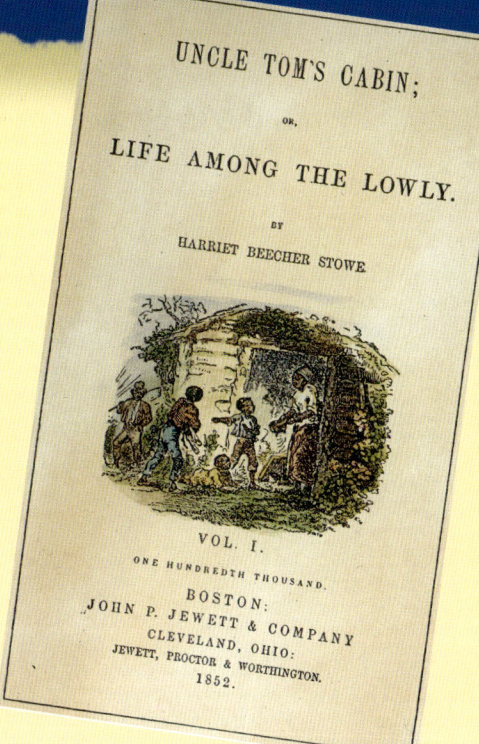

Uncle Tom's Cabin was a book about slaves living in the South. It was an exciting book. Many people liked it. Families read it aloud in the evenings. It showed many people in the North what slavery was like.

The book was banned in much of the South. People there said it was full of lies. But Stowe had based her characters on people she knew. She had heard their stories. She knew the stories were true.

THEY MADE A DIFFERENCE

The Real Uncle Tom?

Josiah Henson was the model for wise Uncle Tom. The real-life Henson was a true hero. Henson was a slave for forty years. He and his family escaped to Canada by way of the Underground Railroad. He wrote his own story in 1849. Then he returned to the South again and again. He helped many other slaves escape to freedom. Henson was always a leader. In his new home in Canada, he started a school to educate former slaves.

CHAPTER 2

A Dangerous New Law

The North and South had many differences. Many people supported the new Fugitive Slave Law. They hoped the new law would hold the nation together. Instead, the law pulled the states further apart.

Laws in the free states protected African Americans. This new law ignored state laws. It let slave catchers hunt slaves anywhere. Slave catchers often used bloodhounds. People called it the "Bloodhound Law."

▲ The Fugitive Slave Law united the abolitionists and made them work harder to help free slaves.

RESISTING SLAVERY

No one was safe. Even free blacks were in danger. Some slave catchers kidnapped free blacks and sold them as slaves.

Abolitionists had to take action. Abolitionists held large meetings. They met in New York, Boston, and Chicago. They vowed not to help the slave catchers.

The Underground Railroad also had to meet the challenge. Members would need to work harder than ever.

In My Opinion

The Fugitive Slave Law

AGAINST: An 1851 antislavery meeting issued strong statements: "#1. Resolved, that we pour out upon the Fugitive Slave Law the fullest measure of our contempt and hate . . . and pledge ourselves to resist it actively as well as passively . . ." William H. Parker, lieutenant in the Confederate Navy

FOR: Some prominent politicians spoke very differently. ". . . in regard to the return of persons bound to service, who have escaped into the free States, . . . it is my judgment that the South is right, and the North is wrong . . . I speak today for the preservation of the Union." Massachusetts Senator Daniel Webster

CHAPTER 3

All Aboard!

What was it like to be a passenger on the Underground Railroad?

Every man or woman had a story. Many began in the same way. After years of bad treatment, a slave was "ready to run." For Jake Williams, the time came when a cruel owner hit his dog with a rock.

In other cases, a slave knew that she or her children would be sold. Or a kind owner died. Caroline Hammond's life changed after her owner died. He was a kind man. His widow was mean. Caroline's father was buying her mother's freedom. The widow refused to accept the last payment.

Eyewitness Account

Caroline Hammond told the story of her family's escape:
"Mother and father and I were concealed in a large wagon drawn by six horses. On our way to Pennsylvania we never alighted on the ground in any community or close to any settlement, fearful of being [caught] by people who were always looking for rewards."

As a result, the family ran away. In Baltimore, Maryland, the UGRR took them in. The widow offered a reward, but it was too late. UGRR agents took the family to safety in Pennsylvania.

Primary Source

Harriet Jacobs was afraid of her cruel owner, but she did not want to leave her children behind. So for seven years she hid in a tiny attic room nearby. Family and friends brought food and news. The roof was so low she could not stand upright. At last, she decided to escape. "I determined to steer for the North Star at all hazards," Jacobs wrote of her story in *Incidents in the Life of a Slave Girl*.

CHAPTER 3

The Long Road to Freedom

The best time for slaves to escape was Saturday night. Sometimes, no one would miss them until Monday. That gave the runaways a head start. A slaveholder could not hire a slave catcher until Monday.

The next weeks were hard. The main UGRR networks were in the free states. Getting there was always dangerous. Runaways were on their own until they reached the border states. Then they hoped to find a UGRR conductor. The conductor would help them reach the North. This journey could take weeks or months.

▲ When slaves reached the borders of the Northern states, they found friends to help them get to Canada.

ALL ABOARD!

Runaways from the deep South took a greater chance. They had an even longer journey. They traveled by night, following the North Star. During the day, they hid in caves, woods, and swamps. They picked nuts, fished, or hunted. With luck, they might find food at a slave cabin. They might hear news, too. Slave catchers and their dogs were never far behind.

Eyewitness Account

Solomon Northrup was born free in New York. In 1841, he was kidnapped, taken south, and sold into slavery. After twelve years, he escaped. He fled into a snake-filled swamp:

"Fear gave me strength. . . . Every few moments I could hear the yelpings of the dogs. They were gaining upon me. Every howl was nearer and nearer. Each moment I expected they would spring upon my back—expected to feel their long teeth sinking into my flesh. There were so many of them. . . . Hope revived a little as I reached the water."

▼ This 1861 painting is called "The Hunted Slave."

CHAPTER 3

Primary Source

Secrecy and trust were the keys to safe passage on the Underground Railroad. In many cases secret seals, or stamps, were used by stationmasters. This was to prevent them from being discovered. The ring in this picture is a seal ring used to make these seals and stamps. Look closely and you will see the drawing of a locomotive. This ring is believed to represent the last U.S. stop on the slaves' journey to Canada and freedom.

UGRR agents had codes and signals. Some signals showed that a house was a safe place. One signal might be a candle in a window. Another signal could be a quilt hung on a fence.

Codes were also hidden in the words of songs, or **spirituals** (SPEER-ih-choo-uhlz). Spirituals were religious folk songs. Many spirituals used symbols of freedom. One song went, "Swing low, sweet chariot, coming for to carry me home." The words seemed to be about heaven. But that "chariot" might also carry a slave to freedom.

ALL ABOARD!

"Passengers" on the Underground Railroad traveled in different ways. Some traveled by night. Some hid in wagons under hay or piles of vegetables. Others wore disguises. A man could wear a woman's black dress and veil. He looked like a widow in mourning. A young woman could cut her hair short and dress as a sailor. Slave catchers looking for a woman would pass her by on the street.

Ellen and William Craft used disguises. Ellen was light-skinned. She dressed as a young white planter. William, her husband, traveled as her servant. To hide her face, Ellen wore glasses and a scarf. She put one arm in a sling. This hid the fact that she could not write. Dressed like this, the couple traveled from Georgia to Pennsylvania. They stayed at good hotels the whole way.

Primary Source

The song "Follow the Drinking Gourd" gave travel directions to fleeing slaves. The "Drinking Gourd" was another name for the Big Dipper, in the northern sky. North was where freedom lay. The song described landmarks, such as hills and rivers. It also advised runaways to reach the Ohio River in winter, when it would be easier to cross on the ice.

CHAPTER 4

Heroes of the Underground Railroad

Escaping slavery took great courage. Working for the UGRR also took courage. Some towns supported conductors and stationmasters. Others did not.

"The Moses of Her People"

Only a few agents traveled into the South to rescue people. They were known as "abductors" (ab-DUHK-terz). The most famous of these agents was Harriet Tubman.

It's a FACT

Harriet Tubman was sometimes called "the Moses of her people." In the Bible, Moses led the ancient Hebrews out of slavery in Egypt. Tubman did the same for African Americans in 19th century America.

◀ Harriet Tubman as a young woman

Tubman was a slave. She was born in Maryland around 1822. As a child, she was hit on the head. She had blackouts the rest of her life. That did not stop her, though.

Tubman escaped to Philadelphia. There she worked with William Still. Then she learned that her family was going to be sold.

To free them, she went back to the South and got them out. Then she went back twelve more times. Tubman was tough on her passengers. She made them stay quiet. She threatened to leave them. But she brought them all to safety. She was never caught.

✓ Point

Read More About It

To learn more about Harriet Tubman, ask your teacher or librarian to help you find information in books or on the Internet.

◀ Harriet Tubman retired to New York. There she told her life story to a writer.

CHAPTER 4

Eyewitness Account

Levi Coffin described how his family was always ready for unexpected visitors:

"We knew not what night or what hour of the night we would be roused from slumber by a gentle rap at the door. That was the signal announcing the arrival of a train of the Underground Railroad. . . . Outside in the cold and rain, there would be a two-horse wagon loaded with fugitives, [most] of them women and children. . . . When they were all safely inside and the door fastened, I would cover the windows, strike a light and build a good fire. By this time my wife would be up and preparing victuals [food] for them, and in a short time the cold and hungry fugitives would be made comfortable."

A Busy "Station"

Levi and Catharine Coffin were Quakers (KWAY-kerz). They hated slavery so much that they left North Carolina. Their new home in Indiana became a well-known UGRR station. It was a busy station. Three UGRR routes crossed there. Sometimes several groups arrived at once. In twenty years, more than 2,000 runaways found food and comfort there.

▲ Built in 1827, the Coffin House is now a National Historic Landmark.

HEROES OF THE UNDERGROUND RAILROAD

▲ This painting by Charles T. Webber shows Levi Coffin, his wife Catharine, and Hannah Haydock helping a group of fugitive slaves.

Local Heroes

Ripley, Ohio, is on the Ohio River. Today, Ripley is a village of about 1,800 people. It was once a major center for the UGRR. For slaves in Kentucky, Ripley meant freedom. Brave townspeople —both black and white— helped many slaves escape.

Fugitives crossing the river looked for a lighted candle. The candle burned in the window of John Rankin's house. John Rankin was a minister. His home was a well-known station on the river. His six sons helped in the work. About 2,000 fugitives found safety there. One conductor said, "It always meant freedom for the slave if he could get to this light."

CHAPTER 4

▲ John Parker wrote that his house "has played its part in concealing men and women seeking a haven of safety."

John Parker was another famous agent in Ripley. Parker was a former slave. After a daring escape, he became an inventor and businessman. He also became a UGRR conductor. Parker helped about 440 fugitives escape. At first, he kept a notebook of their names and homes. Then the Fugitive Slave Law passed. He burned the notebook in the furnace of his ironworks.

HEROES OF THE UNDERGROUND RAILROAD

Eyewitness Account

For more than four years, the light in the Rankin House guided Arnold Gragston, a slave in Kentucky. He first became a UGRR conductor to help a pretty young woman who wanted to cross to Ripley. He was scared, expecting to be caught and beaten:

"I don't know how I ever rowed the boat across the river. The current was strong, and I was trembling. . . . I know I was a long time rowing there in the cold and worrying. . . . Well, pretty soon I saw a tall light, and I remembered what the old lady had told me about looking for that light and rowing to it. I did; and when I got up to it, two men reached down and grabbed her. I started trembling all over again, and praying. Then one of the men took my arm. . . . 'You hungry, boy?' is what he asked me, and if he hadn't been holding me, I think I would have fell backward into the river."

After that, Gragston regularly took boatloads of people across the river. He never saw most of his passengers. They crossed in the dark of night. He worked for four years without getting caught. Then one day, he and his wife crossed the river one more time—and stayed. They settled in Detroit as a free family.

▲ Today the Rankin House is a National Historic Landmark.

Conclusion

▲ These are a few of the people who worked on the Underground Railroad.

For thousands of African American slaves, the Underground Railroad was the road to freedom. The UGRR also brought hope to those still in slavery. Slaves knew that family and friends were living in freedom. During the Civil War, President Abraham Lincoln freed most of the slaves in the South. Then, in 1865, the Thirteenth Amendment ended slavery in the United States. The work of the UGRR was over.

1619	First Africans arrive in Jamestown, Virginia.
1641	Massachusetts colony legalizes slavery.
1775	Pennsylvania Abolition Society is founded.
1780	Pennsylvania is first state to abolish slavery.
1793	First Fugitive Slave Law is passed.
1808	Slave trade legally ends.
1830s	Underground Railroad develops.
1850	New Fugitive Slave Law is passed.
1852	*Uncle Tom's Cabin* is published.
1861	The Civil War begins.
1863	Emancipation Proclamation ends slavery in Confederate states.
1865	Thirteenth Amendment ends slavery in United States.